# Salmon Summer

written and photo-illustrated by **Bruce McMillan**

Houghton Mifflin Company
Boston

*For Alex Shugak Sr.,*
*my Native Alaska friend and guide*

**Kodiak Island, Alaska**

*S*almon Summer was photographed in the Kodiak National Wildlife Refuge. It was made possible through the generous help of my Alaska Native hosts at Larry Matfay's fish camp: Alex B. Shugak Jr.; his father, Alex B. Shugak Sr.; his mother, Georgene Inga; his uncle, "Willie" Shugak; his younger brother, Larry A. Shugak; his grandmother and her husband, Sally and Gene Johansen; his "auntie," Amanda Johansen; and especially his grandmother's uncle (seen on page 16), Hillarion "Larry" Matfay, born in 1907, who passes on to future generations the ways of his people.

On the way to camp my hosts in the town of Kodiak, Alaska, were Elizabeth and "Andy" Dano. Elizabeth, an elementary school teacher, introduced me to this extended family.

The text was reviewed by Dr. Rachel Mason, a cultural anthropologist for the United States Fish and Wildlife Service, Office of Subsistence Management, Anchorage, Alaska; Jeff Leer, an assistant professor at the Alaskan Native Language Center, Fairbanks, Alaska; and Lori Evans, an elementary school teacher.

The book was photographed in July and August 1996. It was shot using a Nikon F4/MF23 with 24, 85, 105 micro, 180, 300, and 600 mm lenses. A polarizing filter was often used when shooting in full sunlight. The 35 mm film, Kodachrome 64, was processed by Kodak at Fair Lawn, New Jersey.

Walter Lorraine  Books

Library of Congress Cataloging-in-Publication Data

McMillan, Bruce.
Salmon summer / written and photo-illustrated by Bruce McMillan
p. cm.        Includes bibliographical references.
Summary: A photo essay describing a young Native Alaska boy fishing for salmon on Kodiak Island as his ancestors have done for generations.
ISBN 0-395-84544-0
1. Salmon fishing—Alaska—Moser Bay (Kodiak Island)—Juvenile literature. 2. Salmon fishing—
Alaska—Moser Bay (Kodiak Island)—Pictorial works—Juvenile literature. [1. Salmon fishing—Alaska.
2. Kodiak Island (Alaska). 3. Indians of North America—Alaska.]
I. Title
SH 684.M35        1998        639.2'756'0916434—dc21
97-29679        CIP        AC

Printed in Singapore    TWP    10  9  8  7  6  5

Design and typesetting by Bruce McMillan.
The text is set in 14-point Palatino.

Summer
Matfay Fish Camp
Moser Bay, Kodiak Island, Alaska

Alex loves to snack on tamuuq *(tah·MOHK)*, chewy dry fish. This tamuuq comes from halibut, his favorite fish to catch. But now that the salmon are running, Alex is going fishing for salmon.

He's been waiting for them to return. As young fry they left the nearby stream to live at sea. To complete their life cycle, they're coming back to the same stream to spawn.

This summer nine-year-old Alex is finally old enough to help his father set the gill net. Like their Aleut *(AL·ee·oot)* ancestors, they catch fish to feed their family.

By next morning the net is full of flapping fish. They are trapped in the almost-invisible mesh of the net as they try to swim past Alex's beach. Alex and his father pull their net. It's time to "pick" fish.

Alex wears gloves to protect his hands not only from the fine mesh of the nets but also from the stings of jellyfish. It's not as much fun as fishing with a line, but there will be time for that later. Now they must finish landing today's catch.

Back on the beach Alex's father asks him if he can tell what kind of salmon they caught. First Alex picks out a humpy, the pink salmon that are running in the greatest numbers. Below that he lays a red salmon, the best kind for eating. Then he lays down a silver salmon and finally, at the bottom, a big dog salmon.

Alex cleans salmon alongside his father as seagulls watch from afar. He uses the same knife his grandmother's uncle used to skin bears. He cuts filets from one of the fish for dinner. With the others, he cuts off the head, pulls out the guts, and leaves the skin and tails on. They're for the smokehouse. But as the cleaned fish hang outside, uninvited visitors fly in to steal a meal.

Magpies sneak in for a bite when nobody's watching. They're not the only hungry birds. Alex leaves salmon scraps to wash away with the tide and be eaten by scavengers. The gulls swoop down for a fish feast. As always, they eat their favorite part of the salmon first—the eyes. At dusk another animal arrives to take home more of Alex's scraps.

A fox slinks by to pick up a meal. She takes it back to her pups in their den near Alex's cabin.

Farther up the bay, at Dog Salmon Creek, a Kodiak bear grabs a king salmon to feed her two cubs. Later, when Alex goes by, the bears are gone. But he knows they were here. He follows claw tracks in the sand and discovers the remains of their meal.

15

There's an abundance of salmon for all. There's salmon for the eagles to catch. There's more salmon for Alex to catch and give to the people in town who are too old to fish.

There's also salmon for the family's smokehouse. The fish Alex and his father cleaned are smoked. Alex hangs the smoked red salmon outside in the sun to cure. The fish drip dry, which removes the excess oil.

Soon the smoked salmon is ready to eat. Alex's little brother, Larry, tears off a bite as he watches Alex clean more fish.

When Alex discards some salmon eggs, it reminds him that there are ripe salmonberries behind camp, and he's hungry. Alex picks berries for jam but eats most of what he picks. Then he and his father head out to the family's crab traps. He brings along a few small salmon for bait.

Alex hauls in the family's shallow-water trap for Dungeness crabs but finds nothing. He slices open some salmon and baits the trap again.

In deeper water he helps his father haul their trap for Alaskan king crabs. He finds one inside, but the prickly crab is too small to keep. Overboard it goes. After Alex rebaits the trap, he helps push it over the side and watches until it sinks out of sight. Then he heads up the bay to Dog Salmon Creek. It's time to play.

It's time to fish for fun. The creek is full of salmon. The fish are heading upstream to mate—to lay and fertilize their eggs on the gravelly bottom. Alex ties a silver lure with three hooks on it to his line. There are so many fish that he often hooks one in its body.

Alex catches fish after fish. But he doesn't keep them. Every time he catches one, he releases it. He knows the biggest fish is yet to come—and it won't be a salmon.

The last salmon Alex catches is a male humpy. He can tell this one's a male because it is changing. Its jaws are becoming hooked. Its back is growing a hump. Its life cycle is almost complete.

All the salmon will soon die upstream after expending their last energy to mate and cover their eggs with gravel. The floating bodies will become easy meals for the wildlife. But not this salmon. This one will be Alex's bait for the biggest fish of all—a halibut.

It's time to head out in the boat and go hooking. It's time to get fish for tamuuq.

Alex baits a hook with his salmon, attaches a heavy sinker, and hangs the line overboard. It drops to the bottom. He waits and feels with his fingers for a tug on the line. He feels a nibble. He pulls. Nothing. He feels another nibble and tugs hard. He's got it. The hook is set. Alex holds on and starts pulling it in.

With help from his father, Alex pulls the halibut aboard. It's almost as big as Alex, and it's not even a very big one.

Back at camp, Alex's grandmother slices the halibut flesh into strips and hangs them up to dry. Alex can hardly wait. It takes about ten days. Finally, the dry fish, his favorite snack, is ready. It's the same kind of snack his ancestors ate—tamuuq.

## Alex's Heritage

Fireweed, a purple wildflower, grows taller than Alex. When the top blossoms, it will be time for him to leave camp. He will move back to the village of Old Harbor on Kodiak Island. Next summer, as his ancestors did before him, he'll return for another season of fishing.

Alaska Natives and all other residents of Kodiak Island may engage in subsistence fishing—noncommercial fishing with specified gear—between 6 AM and 9 PM. When salmon are running, a game warden counts fish as they swim upstream. No commercial fishing is allowed until enough fish have swum by to assure plentiful spawning. However, subsistence fishing is permitted because it doesn't have an adverse impact on future catches.

Alex Shugak (SHOO·gahk) Jr.'s name reflects the history of Kodiak Island. His first name is Russian. In 1784 Russians established the first permanent settlement in Alaska on Kodiak. The United States purchased Alaska from the Russians in 1867 and granted it statehood in 1959. However, the Russian influence endures. For example, many Alaska Natives, and some of Alex's relatives, still practice the Russian Orthodox religion.

Alex's last name, Shugak, is an Alaska Native name. He is Aleut, a term his grandmother's uncle, Hillarion "Larry" Matfay, prefers to call his people. The Russians referred to both Aleutian Islanders and Kodiak Islanders as Aleuts, even though the Kodiak Natives are a different cultural group from the Aleutian Aleuts. A relatively new term for the Kodiak cultural group is Alutiiq (ah·LOO·TIK). This name is recognized by the Alaska Native Language Center and was agreed upon by representatives of Alex's people in the 1980s. Whatever terminology is used, Alex is an Alaska Native with a rich heritage.

# Glossary

**Alaskan king crab** —— a large crab *(Paralithodes camtschatica)* found in deep waters and highly prized for the edible flesh in its legs and claws.

**Alaska Native** —— a person of a cultural group whose ancestors lived in Alaska.

**Aleut** —— the old name (and the name still preferred by many Natives) for Alaska Natives from Kodiak Island and elsewhere. Not to be confused with Aleutian Aleuts.

**Aleutian Aleut** —— an Alaska Native of the cultural group whose ancestors lived on the Aleutian Islands. A different cultural group from Kodiak Island Aleuts.

**Alutiiq** —— the new name (recognized by anthropologists) for Alaska Natives from Kodiak Island and elsewhere. Also the name of their language.

**Dog salmon** —— also called chum salmon *(Oncorhynchus keta)*. It has the widest geographic range of all the Pacific salmon. Prior to spawning, a male develops doglike canine teeth.

**Dungeness crab** —— a medium-size crab *(Cancer magister)* found in shallow waters with edible flesh in the claws, legs, and body.

**Fish camp** —— a group of seasonal huts on the coast where Alaska Native families spend the summer fishing.

**Gill net** —— a mesh net made of fine line that extends out from the shore. Medium-size fish such as salmon are caught in the seemingly invisible "screen wall," while smaller fish easily pass through, and larger fish, unable to enter the mesh's openings, turn back.

**Halibut** —— a large flatfish *(Hippoglossus stenolepis)* sought for eating and often dried to make tamuuq. It's a bottom-dwelling fish that can weigh from 30 to 400 pounds.

**Hook** —— to fish for halibut using a hand line. Tied to the line is a sinker and a large hook that is baited with a chunk of fish.

**Humpy** —— also called pink salmon *(Oncorhynchus gorbuscha)*. It is the most abundant salmon in North America.

**King salmon** —— also called Chinook salmon *(Oncorhynchus tshawytscha)*. It is the largest of the Pacific salmon but also the least abundant. It is Alaska's state fish.

**Kodiak bear** —— a brown bear *(Ursus middendorffi)* that can weigh as much as 1,500 pounds. It may feed on vegetation but prefers salmon.

**Kodiak Island** —— an island off southern Alaska in the Gulf of Alaska. It is 67 miles wide and larger in area than the state of Delaware.

**Life cycle** —— all stages of salmon development beginning with the fertilized egg and ending with death after spawning.

**Magpie** —— also called black-billed magpie *(Pica pica)*. It has a *yak-yak-yak* cry. It may feed on fruit and seeds but prefers to eat meat, including salmon.

**Pick** —— to harvest salmon by pulling trapped fish from the mesh of gill nets.

**Red salmon** —— also called sockeye salmon *(Oncorhynchus nerka)*. It is prized commercially for its deep red flesh. It is often smoked. Because it rarely goes after a fishing lure, few are caught at the end of a fishing line.

**Salmonberry** —— a raspberry-like berry that looks like clusters of small salmon eggs. It has a unique taste and is picked not only to eat fresh but also to make jam and jelly.

**Spawn** —— to lay fish eggs on the gravelly bottom of a stream.

**Subsistence fishing** —— noncommercial fishing by Kodiak Alaska Natives and all other residents of Kodiak Island. Specified fishing gear must be used, such as a gill net. Hours are from 6 AM to 9 PM. Fish may be used by the family or shared, but never sold. Many residents have additional licenses to fish commercially.

**Tamuuq** —— the Alutiiq noun meaning "edible dry fish."

# Bibliography

Armstrong, Robert H. *Alaska's Fish: A Guide to Selected Species*. Seattle: Alaska Northwest Books, 1996.

———. *Guide to the Birds of Alaska*. Seattle: Alaska Northwest Books, 1980.

Boshung, Herbert T., Jr., et al. *The Audubon Society Field Guide to North American Fishes, Whales, and Dolphins*. New York: Alfred A. Knopf, 1983.

Chaffin, Yule, Trisha Hampton Krieger, and Michael Rostad. *Alaska's Konyag Country*. Kodiak, Alaska: Chaffin Incorporated, 1983.

Ehrlich, Paul R., David S. Dobkin, and Darryl Wheye, eds. *The Birder's Handbook: A Field Guide to the Natural History of North American Birds*. New York: Simon and Schuster, 1988.

Field, Nancy, and Sally Machlis. *Discovering Salmon: A Learning and Activity Book*. Middleton, Wisconsin: Dog-Eared Publications, 1993.

Fitzhugh, William W., and Alan Crowell. *Crossroads of Continents: Cultures of Siberia and Alaska*. Washington, D.C.: Smithsonian Institution Press, 1988.

Fobes, Natalie, Tom Jay, and Brad Masten. *Reaching Home: Pacific Salmon, Pacific People*. Seattle: Alaska Northwest Books, 1994.

Gill, Shelly. *Swimmer*. Homer, Alaska: Paws IV Publishing, 1995.

Groot, C., and L. Margolis, eds. *Pacific Salmon Life Histories*. Vancouver: UBC Press, 1991.

Leer, Jeff. *A Conversational Dictionary of Kodiak Alutiiq*. Fairbanks, Alaska: Alaska Native Language Center, 1978.

Mason, Rachel. *The Alutiiq Ethnographic Bibliography*. Kodiak, Alaska: Alaska Humanities Forum, 1995.

Rennick, Penny, ed. *Kodiak*, Vol. 19, No. 3. Anchorage: Alaska Geographic Society, 1992.

Rostad, Michael. *Time to Dance: Life of an Alaska Native*. Anchorage: A.T Publishing, Inc., 1988.

Schofield, Janice J. *Alaska's Wild Plants*. Seattle: Alaska Northwest Books, 1993.

Steelquist, Robert. *Adopt-a-Stream Foundation Field Guide to the Pacific Salmon*. Seattle: Sasquatch Books, 1992.